AF185859

Contents

The legend of King Arthur and the Knights of the Round Table, also known as the Arthurian legend, is set in the late 5th century and is an important part of British culture. Told for centuries, the stories are a mix of history, myth, romance, fairy tale and religion. Here are the legend's most important characters:

ARTHUR

QUEEN GUINEVERE

King Arthur was a legendary king of Britain who fought against the Saxon invaders in the late 5th and early 6th century. After many great battles, Arthur and his Knights of the Round Table finally defeated the Saxons. He built the castle Camelot where he lived with his wife Guinevere.

Guinevere was the beautiful wife of King Arthur. Some people say she had a love affair with Arthur's knight, Sir Lancelot. Other people say she was a good wife and queen to Arthur. Many people think Arthur's punishment of his wife was the beginning of his downfall.

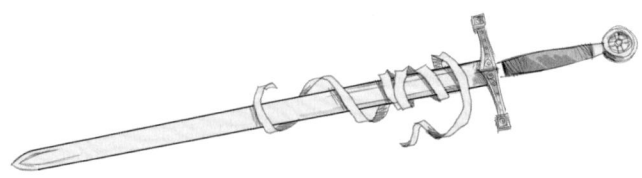

Excalibur was a magical sword with special powers. The owner of the sword could not be wounded or killed. King Arthur was given Excalibur by the Lady of the Lake. Before he died, he asked one of his knights to bring the sword back to the Lady of the Lake.

King Arthur

by
David Fermer

Alles Digitale zu diesem Buch kann auf der Lernplattform
allango von Ernst Klett Sprachen abgerufen werden. So geht's:

QR-Code scannen
oder **www.allango.net**
aufrufen

Buchtitel oder ISBN in
der Suche eingeben und
auf das Buchcover klicken

Zum Inhalt navigieren,
direkt abrufen
oder speichern

Dieses Symbol bedeutet, dass zu einem Buch-Abschnitt
ein digitaler Inhalt verfügbar ist.

Ernst Klett Sprachen
Stuttgart

Digitale Extras:
Zu dieser Geschichte gibt es online (s. die erste Seite des Buches) auch das
Hörbuch und einen Wortschatztrainer für alle Vokabeln im Glossar.

1. Auflage   14 | 2025

Alle Drucke dieser Auflage sind unverändert und können im Unterricht nebeneinander verwendet
werden.
Die letzte Zahl bezeichnet das Jahr des Druckes. Das Werk und seine Teile sind urheberrechtlich
geschützt. Jede Nutzung in anderen als den gesetzlich zugelassenen Fällen bedarf der vorherigen
schriftlichen Einwilligung des Verlags.

© Ernst Klett Sprachen GmbH, Rotebühlstraße 77, 70178 Stuttgart 2014.
Alle Rechte vorbehalten. Die Nutzung der Inhalte für Text- und Data-Mining ist ausdrücklich
vorbehalten und daher untersagt.
www.klett-sprachen.de

Autor: David Fermer
Redaktion: Don Haupt
Layoutkonzeption: Elmar Feuerbach
Umschlaggestaltung: Elmar Feuerbach
Grafik: Matthias Pflügner, Berlin
Tonregie und Schnitt: Andreas Nesic, Stuttgart
Sprecherin: Debby Böhm
Druck und Bindung: Plump Druck & Medien GmbH, Rheinbreitbach

Förderung
nachhaltiger
Waldbewirtschaf

PEFC

PEFC/04-31-3752   www.pefc.de

Printed in Germany
ISBN 978-3-12-572260-6

Merlin was a famous wizard. His mother was a normal woman, but his father was said to be a spirit. It was from him that Merlin got his supernatural powers.

Galahad was Lancelot's son and was known as the "pure knight". He was best known for his success in finding the Holy Grail, the cup used by Jesus at the Last Supper.

Lancelot was the most famous of Arthur's knights. He was Arthur's most trusted knight. Also known as Lancelot of the Lake, he fell in love with Arthur's wife, Guinevere. Lancelot came from Gaul in northern France.

Mordred was King Arthur's nephew and he was one of the Knights of the Round Table. Mordred betrayed Arthur and fought against him at the Battle of Camlann, where he was killed after wounding Arthur.

The towering castle of Tintagel. The wild seas of the Atlantic Ocean. The black cliffs of the coast. Night-time.

In the sky, a storm is brewing. A man in a long white robe walks over the bridge to the castle gates. He walks with a long stick. On top of the staff is the head of a goat.

The soldiers at the castle gates do not speak to him. They do not ask him his name or why he is here. They just open the gates and let the man in.

As the rain begins to fall and a flash of lightning lights up the sky, the man goes into the tower. He goes up the stairs to the king's chambers.

"Welcome, Merlin," King Uther says as the man comes into the room.

The king's wife is asleep in her bed. Her stomach is big and round like a ball. She is pregnant.

"These are bad times to bring a child into the world," Uther tells Merlin. "The chieftains are fighting each other. The Saxons are coming from the east. There is danger everywhere."

Merlin puts his ear to the queen's stomach and listens. "The child will be here tomorrow," he says. "A boy."

"My first son. The future king," says Uther. "They will try to kill him, Merlin. The chieftains will take him away from me. I cannot let that happen."

The woman in the bed is dreaming. She lifts her hand and touches Merlin's face. "Arthur!" she says, her eyes closed. "Arthur, my child!"

"You must take the boy with you," Uther says. "You must make him king when I die."

Merlin puts his hand on the queen's head to calm her. "It will break her heart," he says quietly.

"Yes, it will. But we must do it. To protect the boy and the kingdom. Will you do this for me, Merlin? Will you take my child and make him king?"

Merlin puts his hand on the queen's belly. "You will give him the name of Arthur?" he asks.

The king nods. Merlin touches the queen's stomach with his staff. "Then one day Arthur will be king," he says. Outside lightning strikes again.

Merlin looks into the mirror. His hair is long and grey. His face is wrinkled like the bark of a tree. He is an old man. His life will soon be over.

"Merlin! Merlin!"

A voice outside. Merlin leaves his cave and goes out into the forest. A knight on a brown horse is standing outside the cave.

"Are you the magician Merlin?" the knight asks without getting down from his horse.

Merlin nods. "I am Merlin. But I am not a magician."

"How can I know you are the man you say you are?" the knight asks.

Merlin looks at the man. "Your horse is tired."

The knight shakes his head. "No. My horse is fit and strong," he says.

"You are wrong." Merlin touches the horse's nose. "*Your horse is tired.*"

Suddenly the horse drops to its knees and lies down on the ground to rest. The knight falls off the horse.

"Now do you believe me?" Merlin asks.

"I have a message for you," the knight says, getting up from the ground. "From Tintagel Castle. King Uther is dead."

"I know," Merlin says. "He died this morning."

The knight looks at Merlin in amazement.

Merlin goes over to the Great Rock and looks down to the river. The women are washing clothes. The children are playing. Arthur and Merlin's oldest son are having a sword fight with sticks.

"He is only seventeen," Merlin says. "So young to be king."

"King Uther said that you would tell the chieftains about Arthur," the knight continues. "Shall I send them a message from you?"

"No," Merlin says. "Words are weak. Only actions will bring the chieftains to accept Arthur."

Merlin takes his sword and looks at its blade. "Tell the chieftains that the next king will be chosen here, at the Great Rock." Merlin puts the tip of his sword onto the stone and pushes it into the rock like a knife into butter. "Whoever can pull this sword out of the rock will be king."

" A sword in a stone? How is that possible?" asks Cuthbert.

"It is black magic," says Mordred. "A trick."

"But it is King Uther's wish," says Ethelred. "We must do as Merlin says."

The chieftains meet at the Great Rock in the forest near Tintagel Castle. People from all around the country also come to the rock. Ordinary people. Poor people.

A great silver sword is sticking out of the stone.

Merlin stands next to the stone. "Twenty chieftains are here today," he says. "Whoever pulls the sword out of the stone will be king. Agreed?"

The chieftains raise their swords and shout, "Aye!"

"Before we begin, I must introduce you to someone," Merlin continues. "Someone who will also have a chance to pull the sword out of the stone." Merlin turns to his cave. "Arthur, come here!"

A young man comes out of the cave. The chieftains stare at him in amazement. He looks just like the dead King Uther!

Merlin puts his hand on the boy's shoulder. "This is Uther's son," he says. "Uther gave him to me when he was born. Arthur also has a right to be king, but only if he can pull the sword out of the stone. Agreed?"

The chieftains look at each other. They do not raise their swords. A few say "Aye!", others say nothing. But no one argues with Merlin.

"Then let the competition begin!" calls Merlin.

The first chieftain walks up to the stone. He takes the sword by the handle and pulls. The sword doesn't move at all. He puts both hands on the sword and pulls. Nothing. He jumps onto the stone and pulls again without success. This happens again and again. Twenty chieftains, twenty strong men. None of them can pull the sword out of the stone.

"Arthur, it is your turn now," says Merlin when the chieftains are finished.

Arthur steps up to the stone. He closes his eyes and thinks of his father and mother and pulls the sword out of the stone.

The crowd cheers. "The king!" There is nothing the chieftains can do. "Kneel before your king," Merlin tells them, pointing at the young Arthur. The chieftains look at each other, then they fall to their knees.

The abbey is full of people. Chieftains from all over the country sit at the front of the church with their wives and children. Behind them bishops and monks. Even French and Saxon noblemen are in the abbey.

Arthur walks up the aisle to the throne.

"Arthur, do you promise to rule over this land for the good of its people?" asks the bishop.

Arthur nods. "I do."

"Do you promise to keep the peace and protect the people?"

"I do."

"Then I crown you king," says the bishop.

He lifts the golden crown and places it on Arthur's head.

Music. Singing. Children dance through the abbey. Arthur sits on his throne and watches the festivities. Merlin stands next to him.

"You must be careful," he says to Arthur as they watch the children dance. "Do you see those three chieftains over there?"

Three chieftains are sitting together in the second row, talking.

"Their names are Mordred, Cuthbert and Ethelred," Merlin explains. "The most dangerous of them all is Mordred. One day he will start a rebellion against you and try to take your crown."

"What do you want me to do?" Arthur asks. "I promised to keep the peace."

"Sometimes you must use force to keep the peace," Merlin says. "You need an army. A small but strong one. An army of knights."

"Where will I find these knights?" Arthur asks.

"In France, in Britain," Merlin explains. "You must look for them yourself. If Mordred attacks you, you will be ready."

Arthur nods. "And one more thing: you will need Excalibur," adds Merlin.

"Excalibur?" Arthur looks at Merlin in surprise. "What is that?"

"A magic sword," Merlin explains. "Whoever has it in their hand cannot be hurt. The holder of the sword is invincible."

"And where is this sword?" Arthur asks.

"I will show you tomorrow," says Merlin as the music ends.

A lake in the forest. The water is as flat as a mirror. Two birds fly over the water. They land at the side of the lake.

"Is this the place?" Arthur asks. He is standing by the water with Merlin.

Merlin nods. "Excalibur is in there," he says, looking out over the lake.

"But the lake is huge!" Arthur says. "How can we find it?"

"We must ask the Lady of the Lake," Merlin explains.

Arthur does not ask any more questions. Swords in the water! Ladies in the lake! It's all very mysterious to him.

"Give me your hand," Merlin says. "Close your eyes. What you see in your head will come true."

Arthur closes his eyes. A picture comes into his head. A woman's hand, holding a silver sword, comes out of the water.

The two birds on the side of the lake take off and fly over Arthur's head. They pull out some of Arthur's hair.

"Ouch!" Arthur screams.

The birds fly over the water and drop Arthur's hair into the lake.

On the spot where Arthur's hair lands the water ripples in ever growing circles.
A woman's hand slowly appears holding a sword.
"Excalibur!" says Arthur. "Tell the birds to bring me the sword, Merlin."
Merlin laughs. "The sword is too heavy for the birds."
"Then make the sword as light as a feather," Arthur suggests.
"I am not a magician," says Merlin with a smile. "If you want Excalibur, you will
have to go and get it yourself. Or have you forgotten how to swim?"
"Swim?!" says Arthur. The sun is shining, but it is a cold winter's day. Merlin
laughs. Arthur gets undressed and goes into the ice cold water.
"Merlin! Cc-c-can't you make the water warmer?" he asks, shivering.
Merlin laughs. "Swim, my king, swim!"
Arthur swims to the middle of the lake. He takes the sword out of the Lady's
hand. It's so heavy he can hardly swim with it.
After he has taken the sword, the hand disappears back into the water.
"Now you are invincible," says Merlin at the side of the lake.

" My Lord, why is the table round?" asks Seaton, Arthur's servant.

"Because we are all the same in the eyes of God," Arthur replies.

Seaton looks at his king in surprise. "Can I sit at the table too?"

Arthur laughs. "No, Seaton! This table is for my knights only. Why don't you go and see if they have arrived yet?"

Seaton goes out into the courtyard of Camelot, Arthur's new castle. It has taken him many years to build. The castle is surrounded by high walls and towers.

Arthur's wife, Guinevere, is standing at the palace doors watching the knights ride into the yard.

"I hope they are all noblemen like the king says," Seaton says to her.

Guinevere smiles. "They are knights, Seaton! Of course they are noblemen!"

The knights get off their horses. As they go into the castle they greet the queen. "My Lady ..." they say and kiss her hand.

One of the knights speaks French to her. "Votre Majesté ..." he says as he presses his lips to the back of her hand.

"Welcome, my dear Lancelot!" says Arthur as he comes out of the hall and sees the handsome French knight. "I am glad you are here! I wasn't sure if you would come!"

"But, my Lord, you came all the way to France to find me. The least I can do is come to Britain in return." Lancelot bows to his king. "It is an honour."

Lancelot follows the other knights into the castle.

"He is handsome, is he not?" Arthur says to his wife as they watch Lancelot go into the hall.

"Not as handsome as you are," Guinevere says.

"You flatter me!" says Arthur. "But I am not blind!"

Guinevere kisses Arthur and goes into the castle. Arthur watches her go. He loves his wife, but he knows she is not perfect.

"My Lord, the knights are seated at the Round Table," says Seaton.

"Good, Seaton!" says Arthur. "Then we can begin!"

Arthur and his knights go to war. In the east of the country, the Saxons from the German lands are invading the island of Britain. Arthur and his knights fight back the Saxon invaders. The battles are bloody. Many men die. But thanks to Excalibur, Arthur is invincible.

Arthur and his knights do not fight alone. Arthur asks the chieftains to help him. They bring not only soldiers but also food and gold to pay for the war. Even the chieftains who dislike Arthur come and fight with him. No one wants the Saxons to take their land. Arthur's cousin, Mordred, is the first chieftain to come and fight alongside him.

After a battle in the forests of Wessex, Arthur's army makes a camp for the night. While the men cook and wash, Arthur goes around the camp to talk to his people. The men tell him about their families at home and about the adventures they had on the battlefield. Arthur listens to their stories.

Later that night Arthur walks past Mordred's tent. Mordred's servant is waiting outside. When he sees Arthur he says, "My Lord, please come inside! Mordred would like to talk to you."

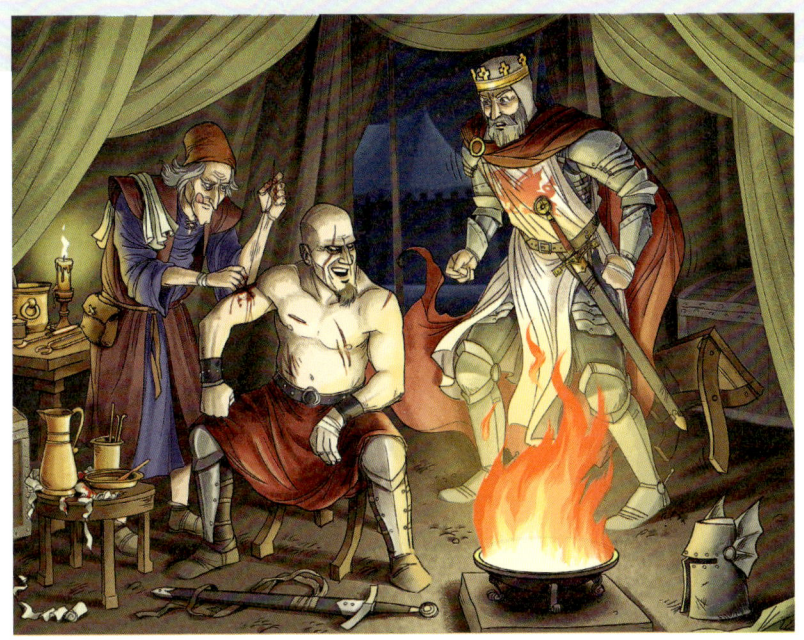

Arthur goes into Mordred's tent. "How goes it, cousin?" Mordred asks.

Mordred is wounded from the battle, but the wound is not bad. A cut on his arm. Mordred asks Arthur to sit with him while his servant cleans the wound and bandages it.

"What is it you want to talk to me about?" Arthur asks.

"I have been watching your knights these last few days," says Mordred, looking into the fire. "Your Frenchman, Lancelot, is a handsome man."

"They are all handsome men," Arthur says. "They have good hearts."

"But Lancelot is particularly handsome," says Mordred. "You know, when I visited you in Camelot last time, I saw him with Guinevere."

"My queen?" Arthur is shocked.

"Yes," Mordred tells him. "I am sorry that it is me who has to tell you this, my Lord, but your queen has betrayed you!"

"You lie!" cries Arthur, but in his heart he knows Mordred speaks the truth. He knew it from the moment Lancelot came to Camelot.

Before Mordred can tell him more, he rushes out of the tent.

Arthur cannot sleep that night. When he closes his eyes, he sees Lancelot and Guinevere together. They hold each other. They kiss. The images in Arthur's head cut his heart like a sword.

The law says that a queen who betrays her king must be punished by death. Arthur does not want Guinevere to die, but the law is the law. If his enemies find out about the betrayal and Arthur doesn't do anything, they will think Arthur is weak.

The next morning King Arthur follows Lancelot down to the river where the knights wash.

"Lancelot! I must speak with you!"

The knight stops what he is doing and listens to the king.

"When did you last go to Camelot?" Arthur asks.

"Some weeks ago," Lancelot replies, surprised by the question.

"Why did I not know about your visit?"

"I went to pick up my new sword from Aerlis the sword-maker."

"Is that all?"

"That is all."

"You were seen with the queen, my wife," Arthur explains.

"Yes, my Lord, I saw her. She was riding her horse," Lancelot explains and adds, curious, "Why do you ask?"

"You held her in your arms!" Arthur says.

"That is a lie!" protests Lancelot. "Was it Mordred who told you this, my Lord?"

"It is not important who told me," Arthur replies. "It is only important if it is true or not."

Lancelot doesn't answer. "Mordred is a dangerous man. He is trying to split up the Knights of the Round Table. Mordred wants to be king."

"Enough!" Arthur takes out his sword. "Mordred is my cousin! He would never want to hurt me."

Lancelot falls to his knees. Arthur stops before he strikes the knight.

"What will you do with Guinevere?" Lancelot asks.

"We will let the court decide!" Arthur declares.

Guinevere stands before the court in the grounds of Camelot Castle. Five bishops sit behind a table. The Knights of the Round Table stand around Guinevere. A crowd of people have come to see the trial.

One of the bishops reads from a piece of parchment. "The court finds you guilty of betraying your king and husband."

People in the crowd whisper to each other, shocked.

"You will be burned at the stake!" says the bishop.

Some people in the crowd shout at the judges. "No! No!" A man runs out of the crowd to help Guinevere, but the knights stop him and push him back.

Queen Guinevere bows her head. She cannot argue with the bishops. It is the law.

King Arthur is watching the trial from the tower. When he hears the bishop announce the punishment, he closes his eyes.

Merlin is standing next to him. "You do not have to do this," he says.

Arthur turns away from the window and goes into his chamber. He cannot watch what will happen next.

Down in the courtyard the knights take Guinevere to a bonfire. They tie her to a wooden stake in the middle of the bonfire.

In his chamber, Arthur puts his hands over his ears. He does not want to hear the screams of the woman he loves as she dies.

The priest comes and says a prayer for Guinevere. Then the knights light the fire. The flames grow around her. She closes her eyes and prays.

But before her dress catches fire, a man on a white horse comes riding into the courtyard and gallops up to the burning bonfire. He is wearing a helmet. The Knights of the Round Table take out their swords to stop him, but in the tower Merlin waves his hand and the knights freeze like ice.

The man cuts the ropes around Guinevere's hands and helps her onto the back of his horse. As the crowd cheers, he rides out of Camelot with the fallen queen. As soon as he is gone, Merlin waves his hand again and the Knights of the Round Table come out of their frozen state. They see the masked man riding into the forest. Although they cannot see his face, they know who he is: Lancelot.

W ithout his queen, King Arthur is only half the man he used to be. Every night he falls asleep thinking of Guinevere. He dreams of their life together. When he wakes, he feels sad and lonely.

Merlin tries to help him, but Arthur can find no happiness in his life. He fights the Saxons until they leave the island. Then he takes his knights to France. He wants to make his kingdom bigger and bigger.

Merlin tells him a bigger kingdom will not help his broken heart, but Arthur does not listen to the old man.

Arthur has Excalibur. He is invincible. Fighting is what he does best.

While fighting in France, Arthur hears about the Holy Grail. One of his knights, Perceval, says that the Holy Grail is somewhere in France. The Holy Grail is the cup which Jesus Christ used at the Last Supper, the cup from which his disciples drank wine, the blood of Christ. People say that the cup has special powers. Arthur wants to find the cup in the hope that its special powers will help him.

He wants to find happiness again.

The Knights of the Round Table help Arthur look for the Holy Grail. Lancelot's son, Galahad, helps him too. Galahad is a knight like his father. He hopes that if he finds the Holy Grail for Arthur, the king will forgive his father and let him return to Camelot. Lancelot is in hiding with Guinevere.

One day, after months of looking for the Holy Grail, Arthur and his knights attack a castle in France. Galahad has information that the Holy Grail is inside the castle. The battle goes on for days. The French knights are strong. Just as Arthur defeats them, he receives a message from Merlin. Merlin writes:

> You must come back to Britain. Mordred has started a rebellion.
> He wants to take your crown. Come soon!

King Arthur has to choose between the Holy Grail and his crown. Before his knights enter the French castle, he stops them.

"Follow me," he tells them. "We must return to Camelot!"

Arthur knows he must kill Mordred. It is the only way to stop him. He returns to Britain with his knights. They camp close to Mordred's castle. They need rest before attacking the castle in the morning.

When Arthur wakes up in the morning, he finds that Excalibur is missing. He calls his servant Seaton, but Seaton is dead.

Murdered.

Someone has stolen Excalibur!

Arthur and his knights go into battle against Mordred's army. Arthur fights like a dog. He sees Mordred on his horse. Excalibur is in Mordred's hand.

"Get off your horse and fight like a man!" Arthur calls to him. Arthur knows that as long as Mordred has Excalibur in his hands, he cannot hurt him.

Mordred gets off his horse. The two men fight. Their swords are long and heavy. They hold them with both hands. Arthur does not try to hit Mordred. He tries to knock Excalibur out of Mordred's hands. Arthur defends himself from Mordred's sword, blocking blow after blow.

Mordred strikes Arthur in the side. Blood runs down Arthur's stomach and legs, but Arthur can fight on.

Striking Excalibur with all his strength, Arthur manages to knock the sword out of Mordred's hand. Now is his chance. He raises his sword and brings it down onto Mordred's shoulder. Mordred falls to the ground, dead.

Arthur is victorious, but he is badly wounded.

"Sire, let me see your wound," says Galahad.

Galahad takes off Arthur's armour and looks at the wound. It is deep.

"We will take you to a doctor," says Galahad.

Arthur puts his fingers to Galahad's lips. "No! No doctor."

"But ...!"

Arthur interrupts him. "Take Excalibur," he says. "Throw it back into the lake where it came from. And go to your father. Tell him that I am sorry. Ask him to look after Guinevere for me. He must forgive me."

"I will, my Lord," Galahad says.

Then Arthur closes his eyes. Galahad feels the king's last breath on his cheek.

Episode twelve

The Knights of the Round Table clean their king's wound and wrap him in a white sheet. A boat is waiting on the river outside Camelot. The knights carry their dead king to the boat.

Merlin's three daughters are waiting on the boat. They take Arthur's body and put him onto a bed of flowers.

"Where are you taking him?" asks Galahad as the women untie the boat.

"To the Isle of Avalon," they answer. "To paradise."

Galahad watches as the women push the boat away from the landing. They float down the river like angels.

Galahad goes back to his horse and rides to the forest. Merlin has told him where to find the lake.

When he arrives at the lake, it has started to rain. It is as if the sky is crying, thinks Galahad. The raindrops fall into the lake, but the surface of the water remains as smooth as a mirror.

Galahad takes out the sword. "You are the sword that killed our king," he says to Excalibur. "Now you must go back to where you came from."

Galahad holds up the sword. "Lady of the Lake!" he calls. "Where are you?"
In the middle of the lake, a hand comes out of the water.
"Take this sword," says Galahad. "May it never again see the light of day."
He throws the sword into the air. It flies across the lake like a bird and lands
in the woman's hand.

On the Isle of Avalon, Merlin's daughters put King Arthur
into his grave. They cover the grave with a great stone.
On the stone are the words:

HERE LIES KING ARTHUR
A FAIR AND NOBLE KING

THE END

Additional information

 The truth behind the legend

In Britain, there is an old castle on the rocky coast of the county of Cornwall in south-west England called Tintagel Castle. Today, Tintagel is a ruin, but it is still an impressive sight, standing on the rocks over the Atlantic Ocean, dark cliffs and wild waters all around it. According to the Arthurian legend, this is the place where King Arthur was born.

The King Arthur we know today is a mixture of different legends, written by different authors at different times. His name first appeared in a book called the "History of the Britons" written in 830 by a Welsh monk called Nennius, who lived in Wales, outside of the Anglo-Saxon kingdom. His "History of the Britons" was therefore full of stories of the triumphs of the Welsh and the other Celtic Britons against their new masters. One of the warriors he wrote about was a man called Arthur.

Centuries later, another man of the church called Geoffrey Monmouth wrote the first full account of Arthur's life in a book called "The History of the Kings of Britain" which he finished in 1138. Geoffrey said his book was based on a lost Celtic manuscript that only he was able to examine. In this work, Arthur's whole life is told for the first time – from his birth at Tintagel to his final betrayal and death. Many of the well-known characters already appear, including Guinevere and Merlin. Geoffrey also mentions the legendary sword, Caliburn (Excalibur), and even the king's final resting place at Avalon. Today, over 200 manuscripts still exist. Geoffrey had a clever way of mixing fact with fiction and making a myth out of history. His book was very successful but what he wrote was far from the truth.

By the time the Tudor King Henry VII came to the throne in 1485, the heroic stories of Arthur's adventures had inspired many more writers and poets to write their own versions of the Arthurian legend, and Arthur was a well-established British hero. Today, we cannot say whether King Arthur ever actually lived or not. There were probably many Arthurs at the time. The Arthurian legend is not really their story. It is the story people at the time wanted it to be.

The times of King Arthur

Europe in the 5th century did not look like the Europe of today. It was not made up of different countries like France, Germany and Spain. It was made up of tribes, from the Angles in today's Denmark to the Visigoths in southern France. There were no official countries, no real borders. Germany did not exist. Britain was an island but not a state. For centuries, the Romans had ruled over Western Europe, bringing system and structure to daily life. In 43 AD, the Romans conquered Britain, fighting back the local tribes, known as the Celts, into Scotland and Ireland and building a gigantic wall called Hadrian's Wall to keep them out.

The Romans stayed in England for several centuries, building many cities, including London, but at the beginning of the 5th Century, the Romans began to leave, as the Roman Empire started to shrink. When the Romans left, other armies began to invade the British Isles. The Danes came from Denmark, and the Saxons came from today's Germany. It is in this period of war that the legend of King Arthur is set.

It is difficult to say how much of the Arthurian legend is true, but it does seem likely that the English chieftains organised an army to keep the Saxons and the Danes out. However, by the end of the 6th century, England had been taken over by the Angles and the Saxons. Anglo-Saxon kings went on to rule over England until the Norman Conquest in 1066.

King Arthur's successful battles against foreign invaders have made him a symbol of Britain's independence. Therefore, people look to the Arthurian legend for inspiration at times of war.

Exercises

Episode 1

Choose the correct answer.

1. Merlin goes up the stairs…
   - a) ☐ to the king's chat room.
   - b) ☐ to the king's chambers.
   - c) ☐ to the king's bathroom.

2. The chieftains will…
   - a) ☐ try to kill Arthur.
   - b) ☐ make Arthur king.
   - c) ☐ organise a surprise party.

3. The queen is…
   - a) ☐ reading in her bed.
   - b) ☐ sleeping in her bed.
   - c) ☐ sleeping on the sofa.

4. The Saxons are…
   - a) ☐ going east.
   - b) ☐ going west.
   - c) ☐ going south.

Episode 2

There is a mistake in each of the following sentences. Find the wrong keywords and write down the correct words.

1. Merlin looks into his pocket. _____

2. Merlin leaves his grave and goes out into the forest. _____

3. The knight looks at Merlin in horror. _____

4. The knight thinks that Merlin is a musician. _____

5. Only actions will bring the children to accept Arthur. _____

6. Whoever can pull this staff out of the rock will be king. _____

Episode 3

Put the sentences into the right order.

sword a out the silver is of great stone sticking.

_____

the pulls handle takes first sword by the chieftain and the.

_____

of of stone the them can the pull none sword out.

_____

tells their Merlin kneel the king chieftains before to.

_____

Episode 4   Crossword

Across
2. opposite of war 6. queen's husband 7. impossible to defeat 8. a knight's weapon
9. *verletzt* (engl.) 11. early invaders of Britain: Anglo-...

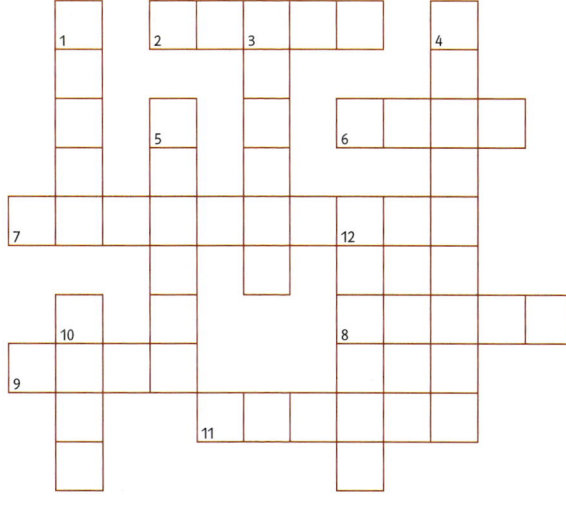

Down
1. what a king wears on his head
3. *angreifen* (engl.)
4. not safe, risky
5. a soldier on a horse
10. to run a country
12. a priest of high rank

Episode 5

Read episodes 3 – 5 again and have a look at the following speech bubbles. Who says this? Write down the names of the characters.

How is
that possible?

Now
you are invincible.

_____

_____

Tell the
birds to bring me
the sword.

Do you
promise to keep
the peace?

_____

_____

It's
black magic, a trick.

_____

Episode 6

Matcher: Who's who and what's what?

1. Arthur _____
2. Guinevere _____
3. Seaton _____
4. Mordred _____
5. Lancelot _____
6. Camelot _____
7. Excalibur _____
8. Merlin _____

sword
castle
knight
magician
king
chieftain
queen
servant

Episode 7

Read the summary and fill in the missing words in their correct form.

to bandage – to betray – bloody – to invade – truth – wounded –
to make a camp – tent – to fight – battlefield – handsome

The Saxons are _____ the island of Britain. Arthur and his knights _____ back the invaders. The chieftains help Arthur but the battles are _____.

After the battle they _____ for the night. The soldiers tell Arthur about the adventures they had on the _____. Later that night Arthur goes into Mordred's _____. Mordred is _____. A cut on his arm. His servant cleans the wound and _____ it.

Mordred thinks that Lancelot is particularly _____ and that the queen has _____ Arthur. In his heart Arthur knows that Mordred speaks the _____.

Episode 8

Complete the mind map: Read episode 8 again and find seven verbs that are like the verb *say*, e.g. *talk*, *speak*, etc.

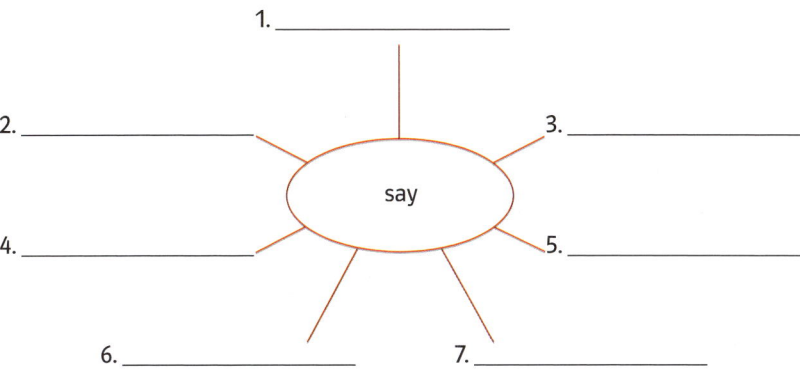

1. _____

2. _____

3. _____

say

4. _____

5. _____

6. _____

7. _____

Exercises

Episode 9

True or false? Circle the answer.

There are six bishops sitting behind a table.	T / F
The court finds Guinevere guilty of betraying her husband.	T / F
Guinevere will be put to prison for the rest of her life.	T / F
A woman tries to help Guinevere, but the knights stop her.	T / F
Merlin and Arthur are watching the trial from the tower.	T / F
The knights tie the bishop to a wooden stake.	T / F
Arthur is very sad because he loves Guinevere.	T / F
Lancelot comes riding into the courtyard on his black horse.	T / F
Merlin waves his hand and stops the knights from attacking Lancelot.	T / F
Guinevere and Lancelot manage to escape.	T / F

Episode 10

What happens first? Put these sentences into the correct order.

a) ☐ Arthur receives a message from Merlin.

b) ☐ Mordred has started a rebellion. He wants to be king.

c) ☐ Arthur and his knights go back to Camelot.

d) ☐ Arthur fights the Saxons until they leave the island.

e) ☐ Galahad hopes that Arthur will forgive Lancelot if he finds the Grail for him.

f) ☐ Arthur and his knights go to France.

g) ☐ Perceval tells Arthur that he can find the Holy Grail in France.

Episode 11

Match the sentence halves.

1. Arthur and his knights go into	a) and looks at his wound.
2. In the morning, Arthur	b) Arthur in the side.
3. Mordred strikes	c) the sword out of Mordred's hand.
4. Get off your	d) Britain with his knights.
5. Galahad takes off Arthur's armour	e) finds that Excalibur is missing.
6. Arthur returns to	f) horse and fight like a man.
7. Mordred falls	g) last breath on his cheek.
8. Galahad feels Arthur's	h) battle against Mordred's army.
9. Arthur manages to knock	i) to the ground, dead.

Episode 12

Fill in the right preposition:

across – up – out – onto – into – in – to – down

1. They wrap the king _____ a white sheet.

2. They carry him _____ the boat.

3. Merlin's daughters put his body _____ a bed of flowers.

4. They float _____ the river like angels.

5. Raindrops fall _____ the lake.

6. Galahad holds _____ the sword.

7. A hand comes _____ of the water.

8. The sword flies _____ the lake.

Glossary

The characters

legend ['ledʒənd] Legende
Knights of the Round Table Ritter der Tafelrunde
myth Mythos
romance Romantik
fairy tale Märchen
legendary legendär
Saxon Angelsachse
invader [ɪn'veɪdə] Angreifer, Eindringling
love affair Affäre
punishment Bestrafung
downfall Untergang
magical magisch
sword [sɔːd] Schwert
wizard Zauberer
spirit Geist
supernatural übernatürlich
powers *hier:* Fähigkeiten
pure [pjʊə] rein
the Holy Grail der Heilige Gral
trusted getreu
Gaul [gɔːl] Gallien
to betray verraten, hintergehen
to wound [wuːnd] verletzen

Episode 1

towering hoch aufragend
to brew [bruː] sich zusammenbrauen
robe Gewand
gate [geɪt] Tor
staff Stock
goat [gəʊt] Ziege

flash of lightning Blitz
chamber ['tʃeɪmbə] Schlafgemach
pregnant schwanger
chieftain *hier:* Anführer
to take away wegnehmen
to lift heben
to touch berühren
to protect beschützen
kingdom Königreich
belly Bauch
to strike [straɪk] *hier:* einschlagen

Episode 2

wrinkled faltig
bark Baumrinde
forest Wald
magician [mə'dʒɪʃn] Zauberer
to drop fallen (lassen), sinken
to lie down sich hinlegen
to rest sich ausruhen
amazement [ə'meɪzmənt] Erstaunen, Verwunderung
to accept akzeptieren
blade [bleɪd] Klinge
tip Spitze
stone Stein
to pull out herausziehen

Episode 3

ordinary gewöhnlich, normal
to stick out of herausragen
Agreed? Einverstanden?
to introduce vorstellen
chance Gelegenheit
to stare anstarren
to raise [reɪz] erheben

to argue with sb [ˈɑːgjuː] mit jdm streiten
handle Griff
none [nʌn] keiner
to step schreiten
to kneel knien

Episode 4
abbey [ˈæbi] Abtei
bishop Bischof
monk Mönch
nobleman Adliger, Edelmann
aisle [aɪl] Gang
to rule regieren, herrschen
for the good of zum Wohl von
peace Frieden
to crown krönen
crown Krone
festivities Feierlichkeiten
row Reihe
rebellion Rebellion
force Gewalt
holder Besitzer
invincible unbesiegbar

Episode 5
flat flach
huge [hjuːdʒ] riesengroß
mysterious mysteriös, geheimnisvoll
spot Stelle, Ort
to ripple Wellen schlagen
to appear auftauchen, erscheinen
as light as a feather federleicht
to shiver zittern

Episode 6
courtyard Hof, Innenhof
surrounded umgeben
to press drücken
handsome gut aussehend
in return als Gegenleistung
to bow [baʊ] sich verbeugen
honour [ˈɒnə] Ehre
to flatter sb jdm schmeicheln
blind [blaɪnd] blind
to be seated sitzen

Episode 7
war Krieg
to invade [ɪnˈveɪd] einmarschieren
bloody [ˈblʌdi] blutig
to dislike nicht mögen
alongside *hier:* an seiner Seite
camp Lager
battlefield Schlachtfeld
tent Zelt
cut *hier:* Schnittwunde
to bandage verbinden
particular besonders
truth Wahrheit

Episode 8
image Bild, Vorstellung
law [lɔː] Gesetz
to punish [ˈpʌnɪʃ] bestrafen
betrayal [bɪˈtreɪəl] Verrat
to protest protestieren, beteuern
to strike [straɪk] schlagen
court [kɔːt] Gericht
to declare erklären

Episode 9

trial Prozess
parchment [ˈpɑːtʃmənt] Pergament
guilty [ˈɡɪlti] schuldig
to whisper flüstern
stake [steɪk] Pfahl
to announce *hier:* verkünden
bonfire *hier:* Scheiterhaufen
prayer Gebet
to pray beten
to catch fire Feuer fangen
to freeze erstarren
rope Seil
state Zustand

Episode 10

he used to be der er früher einmal war
disciple [dɪˈsaɪpl] Jünger
wine [waɪn] Wein
to forgive vergeben
to be in hiding sich versteckt halten
to receive [rɪˈsiːv] erhalten, bekommen

Episode 11

murdered [ˈmɜːdəd] ermordet
to knock *hier:* schlagen
to defend verteidigen
blow Schlag, Hieb
strength Kraft
victorious siegreich
armour [ˈɑːmə] Rüstung
to interrupt unterbrechen
breath [breθ] Atemzug
cheek Wange

Episode 12

to wrap einwickeln
sheet Laken
to untie losbinden
landing *hier:* Anlegeplatz
to float [fləʊt] treiben
angel Engel
surface [ˈsɜːfɪs] Oberfläche
grave [ɡreɪv] Grab
to cover [ˈkʌvə] bedecken, abdecken

Additional information

county Grafschaft
impressive beeindruckend
according to laut, zufolge
triumph [ˈtraɪəmf] Sieg, Triumph
account Bericht
based on basierend auf
heroic heldenhaft
to inspire [ɪnˈspaɪə] inspirieren
well-established bekannt, etabliert

to conquer [ˈkɒŋkə] erobern
several einige, mehrere
including einschließlich
to shrink schrumpfen
period [ˈpɪəriəd] Periode, Zeitraum
likely wahrscheinlich
to take over übernehmen
successful erfolgreich